DEAR BLACK WOMAN
Say a Little Prayer

Also by Revonne Johnson

Dear Black Woman, Tip Yo' Hat

Dear Black Woman, Shine Your Light

Dear Black Woman, Quarantine 2020

Dear Black Woman

Our Side, Our Truth

DEAR BLACK WOMAN
Say a Little Prayer

REVONNE JOHNSON
Poems

Revonne Johnson books are available at quantity discounts with bulk purchase for educational, business, or promotional use. Please use contact information found on the author's website.

www.revonnejohnsonbooks.com

ISBN: 9798883153265

Cover design created by Revonne Johnson using canva.com.

for my mother Inell Leach . . .
she always prayed for me

Contents

Author's Note

      This poetry collection is the fifth book in the *Dear Black Woman* poetry series. It was written in the year 2023, a year that brought an upheaval of emotional events that began in January with the unexpected and traumatic death of my father, a death that was exacerbated by the negligence of the city he served for over four decades. This same period was darkened by the untimely deaths of several hometown friends. It was odd to be surrounded by so much death in such a short period of time. Was God sending a message and putting the rest of us on notice? I didn't have the answer then and I don't have the answer now. So, to help channel some of my feelings of grief, helplessness, and frustration, I decided to personalize this collection—more than usual, capturing my reaction to some impactful global events. This collection also became a poetic healing agent, allowing me to face emotions linked to family traumas and to life in my hometown of Yazoo City, Mississippi.

      Of course, I still focus on the accomplishments of the Black woman and the challenges that we continue to face. I recognize the women leading the charge against former President Donald Trump and his January 6th conspirators. I spotlight female athletes that were dominant in their respective sports, including Coco Gauff, Angel Reese, and ShaCarrie Richardson. I acknowledge recent events that left indelible impacts on my psyche. One of the more memorable events of 2023 was the Montgomery, Alabama Riverfront brawl—the day Black folks fought back. I also attempt to capture the realities of war in 2023 and the pain of watching innocent civilians suffer in the name of religion. The continued degradation of the truth, both online and on air—day after day, remained unsettling as negativity, anger, and fear continued to shroud all aspects of daily life. Despite the childlike behavior of our politicians being layered on top of the ongoing epidemic of gun violence and the undeniable effects of climate change—I can still say that not all was hopeless. There were times of celebration.

The last section of the book is reserved for *Dear Black Woman Reader Spotlight* honorees. These everyday women were highlighted during Black History Month for achievements in their profession, for impacts in their community, and/or for a personal accomplishment/milestone. Each woman has a short bio and a self-titled, six-line, 34-syllable poem that reflects her story. These poems follow the structure of haiku poetry. Haiku poems are meant to paint a vivid picture in very few words. These poems have a 5-7-5 syllable structure—five syllables in the first line, seven syllables in the second line, and five syllables in the third line. Each poem is my attempt to capture the essence of each woman.

I hope that this poetry collection helps you see the world from the unique perspective of Black women, the world as it was in 2023. I also hope that this poetry collection helps you acknowledge and appreciate the life that you have—no matter the circumstances. People all over the world are suffering, and if you stop long enough to listen to someone else's story, you will find that you are truly blessed. The hate and anger for those less powerful, for those who are different, is growing. It's too much! Our democracy and our humanity are at risk. Black women are pushing back, doing their part, but more is needed. The world needs prayer.

Let's pray together.

God shapes the world by prayer. The more praying there is in the world the better the world will be, the mightier the forces against evil.

—Mother Teresa

Section I
Worries of the World

Not Done

Dear Black Woman

I know what they say.
I know what they write.
But you know
            what you must continue to do.
Push aside your doubt and the cold-hearted
dismissals of friends and strangers.
Disregard the naysayers and the "no ways."
Trudge on with your light and your attitude
for you are not done.
Racial injustice, social injustice, political foolery,
and financial inequality
fuel an epidemic of self-serving, self-centered,
and sanctimonious wallowing.
This darkness swarms and swallows the innocent.
My children still need you.
They will follow your lead. They will.
Just continue your work—a journey
of righteousness and rightfulness.
Continue pulling them up . . . and out.
Continue guiding them with your light,
and remember . . .
            you are not alone
            and you are not done.

Your Creator

Uncertainty

hesitant and helpless

as dark days

seem a little darker

      for so many

war in your name

doesn't feel like you

destruction just because

doesn't feel like you

      hunger amidst privilege

      innocence reincarnated

      vigilance invigorated

doesn't feel like you

tomorrow is welcomed

      but what will it bring?

hope or hate?

When the Hat Went Up

Remembering the Montgomery, Alabama Riverfront brawl.

When the hat went up on the dock in Alabama
       ancestors of slaves fought back.

When the hat went up, we fought years of disrespect,
disenfranchisement, and demonization.

When the hat went up, we backed up, and stood up
with our heads up cause we were fed up.

When the hat went up, oppressors watched their
greatest fear—retaliation and condemnation.

When the hat went up, our ancestors cheered our
courage and our choice.

When the hat went up, our communities celebrated
unity with an unspoken understanding.

When the hat went up, there was pride and
vindication—for just a brief moment.

When the hat went up, we were simply asking for what
we were due, for what we have always wanted . . .

       freedom & respect
       life without physical & psychological chains
       and . . .
              an even playing field.

When the hat went up, we did not sit still and endure
their wrath. We fought. We swam. We swung.

When the hat went up . . .
       we had hope.

Don't You

The sting of a bee
is painful. Don't fight the hive . . .
cause you will not win!

When Will Women Give Up

Acknowledging the continued assault on women's reproductive rights.

When will women give up "My body, My choice"
When will women give up their reproductive voice
When will women give up restoring Roe v. Wade
When will women give up?

When a man has a baby!

Three stolen Supreme Court Justices, not enough
Multiple states with *no exception* bans, obviously unjust
States with no clinics, don't care about us
Texas Republicans, still passing crazy stuff
Criminalizing mothers, putting them in cuffs
Blocking approved medications, undeniably corrupt
All part of the fuss and yet still . . . not enough

When will women give up "My body, My choice"
When will women give up their reproductive voice
When will women give up restoring Roe v. Wade
When will women give up?

When a man has a baby!

You'll Be OK

Acknowledging Dr. Claudine Gay's 6-month tenure as Harvard's first
Black president and second female president.

Dr. Gay,
you'll be OK.

This is not new
for women like me and you.

You did nothing wrong.
You belong

in the President's chair.
Harvard put you there

then in the blink of an eye
you had to say good-bye.

You were betrayed
in the worst kind of way

but double standards are common
for every Black woman.

Just take a breath
and stay true to yourself

cause Dr. Gay,
you'll be OK.

When Jaylen Stood Up

Remembering Jaylen Burns, the Jackson State University student who was shot on campus in the fall of 2023.

When Jaylen stood up

  on the campus of JSU

Jaylen was a student leader

  who was well respected.

He was the student leader

  shot while protecting

fellow students

  in an on-campus dorm.

His friend needed a favor.

  So, Jaylen came along.

When Jaylen stood up

  on the campus of JSU

a relationship breakup

  resulted in a feud.

A visitor in the dorm

  had a gun for protection.

Jaylen was a student leader

  who was well respected.

He jumped in the middle

  trying to stop a fight

but in the end was the one

  shot in the dorm that night.

He stood up

    for what was right.

He stood up

    and lost his life,

while saving another's life,

    while saving a brother's life.

His legacy will remain

    rooted in truth

because he stood up

    on the campus of JSU.

The Cover Up

Clothing choices have become more revealing and can often block the rays of inner beauty.

My Daughters,

My heart aches as I watch your unbridled

transformation. Your sign has changed.

It reads . . . *easy.*

Now, there is pollution in your temple.

Confusion, delusion, perfusion, and

a dwindling sense of self-worth

clutter your presence and perception.

Your sign now welcomes all

with no restrictions, no protections, and no limits,

where it once required

respect, credentials, positive intent, and purpose.

Twerking, twisting, stripping, and dropping

what you got for anybody, anywhere for a few *Likes*

by folks that don't know you or like you

        is beneath you.

Why wear the clingy, one size fits all, stretch dress

with no support

    with everything jiggling & wiggling

        under entrenched panty lines

Take care of business before you leave home.
Look to the great women of the past for guidance.
What you wear is who you are—a message to
those approaching your temple.

Those wanting to visit
        should look into your eyes
                before looking down

        at your boobs
                as they play peek-a-boo with the public
        or at the tattoo
                bouncing up and down on your inner thigh.

Don't leave the door open, the windows up, or
the curtains pulled back
for spectators, passer-byers, and strangers to see
that you are special.

No Pretending

Golden shovel poem that borrows the first three lines
from the Langston Hughes poem "I, Too."

You know who **I**
am. I have history **too**
You heard me **sing**
as I built **America**
You know who **I**
am, the backbone of a nation. I **am**
the backbone of a nation trying to hide **the**
the brutal suffering of its **darker**
people—every father, mother, sister, and **brother**
The descendants of slaves know that **they**
can educate and **send**
their children to any school to beco**me**
community leaders and contributors **to**
society. They know that racism is still a thr**eat**
So they will not allow Black history to be rewritten **in**
American history books so that **the**
Master can pretend that we wanted to be in the **kitchen**

Our Reason

Golden shovel poem that borrows the first verse
from Audre Lorde's poem, "Echoes."

Why can't **there**
be a celebration that **is**
just for me? I want **a**
woman's voice with the **timbre**
of Whitney to be pro**of**
that my **voice**
is worthy and **that**
truth **comes**
often **from**
those **not**
included because **being**
dismissed and not **heard**
is hurtful **and**
not **knowing**

that **you**
definitely **are**
more than you are **not**
that just **being**
recognized and **heard**

is being **noticed**
by not **only**
your ba**by**
but **others**

who are **not**
as open to being **heard**
from someone like you. My voice is **for**
all Black women because all **the**
women like me want the **same**
thing—respect. So we ask for this **reason**.

Living Kinless

*Golden shovel poem that borrows the second verse
from Maya Angelou's poem, "On Aging."*

Sometimes I sit and wonder . . . **when**
I die, who will be **my**
caregiver, making sure my **bones**
are laid to rest? Family and friends **are**
not an option for me. My ma**stiff**
Charlie is my nightly companion **and**
he comforts me when an **aching**
heart meets loneliness late at night **and**
my blood pressure is high and **my**
sugar is too and my **feet**
swell when I **won't**
put down the apple pie and **climb**
the stairs instead. Being **the**
Black woman sitting alone on the **stair**
is not who I am. For **I**
have kinless supporters who **will**
care for me. They are the **only**
family that I have. So if I **ask**
they will come **one**
by one. Ready to do any **favor**
so that I **don't**
feel alone or die alone. They **bring**
concern and love to **me**
letting me know that **no**
DNA sample will be needed when I am **rocking**
back and forth in my kitchen **chair**

WCNFS

New category given to children taken to the hospital in Gaza,
"Wounded Child No Family Survivors."

The Beast

For the sexual assault victims of war. So many untold stories of horror.

    The beast
lives in a dark, dismal, and depressing space
where the unthinkable rests
where the unimaginable is imagined
where the unholy thrives
where inhumane behaviors are reasonable
    The beast
drags innocent bystanders
men, women, and children
into an existence of inconsolable suffering
where decency and trust are
                ravaged, raped, and ruined
where victims never come back the same . . .
            if they come back at all
I cry for them; for their anguish; for their sorrow
subjected to a cruelty that is callous
protected by a mind that has intentionally
         purposely, and instinctively forgotten
    The beast
is without a heart, mind, or soul
It does not care. It cannot care. It will never care
It hates and hurts the vulnerable because . . .
    it can

R e a g a n is the pride of an

E r o d e d and fading

P o l i t i c a l party that has been

U n d e r attack

B y Maga extremists who

L o v e 'The Don'

I t is inconceivable that

C h r i s t i a n s, or so-called believers

A r e so accepting of a

N a r c i s i s t

Matt and Kevin

Remembering the insanity that ensued when Kevin McCarthy was elected as the new Speaker of the House.

Matt and Kevin sittin' in a tree

K – I – S – S – I – N – G

After 15 tries, Kevin was king

K – I – S – S – I – N – G

Then Matt got mad and told Kevin to leave

O – U – S – T – I – N – G

No more Speaker for Kevin the King

O – U – S – T – I – N – G

PORTRAIT OF A PRESIDENT

88 charges
44 federal and 44 state
1ST President to be indicted
4 criminal cases

ELECTION INTERFERENCE
Indicted by the STATE OF GEORGIA

ELECTION INTERFERENCE
Indicted by the DOJ

CLASSIFIED DOCUMENTS
in his Florida home
some stacked, some tucked away

Plus, his HUSH MONEY SCHEME
got the attention of the
Manhattan DA

cause he falsified business records
to make Stormy shut up
and go away

88 charges
4 criminal cases
American history
in the making

What is IT?

Colonizers created it

Civil Rights tried to bury it

Black Power fought it

Reagan revived it

Obama reignited it

Trump uncovered it

Corona suspended it

George Floyd's death proved it

The Supreme Court upheld it

January 6th rioters went to jail for it

The Republican party loved it

And now . . .

America can't get rid of IT!

D o n ' t assume that

E v e r y independent voter is

M a d with Trump

O r that all people of

C o l o r will automatically

R e g i s t e r to vote for

A n o t h e r white guy

T r y i n g to stay in power

I Wonder

Climate change is no longer a future threat. In 2023, Earth's average surface temperature was the warmest on record.

2023

likely

the hottest year

on record

and still some

do not believe

science is

trying

but many still not buying

so more is being said

than done

I wonder

       have we missed

       our window?

              . . . to turn it down

              . . . to turn things around

              . . . to help the planet rebound

I wonder

       have we missed

       our window?

The Joke Book

Joke #1:

Your

Student

Loan

Has

Been

Forgiven

Joke #2:

White

Privilege

Is

Not

Real

Joke #3:

Banned

Books

Are

Bad

Joke #4

The

Supreme

Court

Joke #5:

The

Republican

Party

AI Puzzle

Recognizing the growing Artificial Intelligence (AI) revolution and how humanity, technology, and cinema have intersected. 12 movies involving AI technology are hidden in the puzzle below.

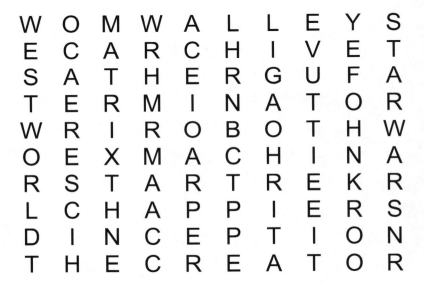

```
W  O  M  W  A  L  L  E  Y  S
E  C  A  R  C  H  I  V  E  T
S  A  T  H  E  R  G  U  F  A
T  E  R  M  I  N  A  T  O  R
W  R  I  R  O  B  O  T  H  W
O  E  X  M  A  C  H  I  N  A
R  S  T  A  R  T  R  E  K  R
L  C  H  A  P  P  I  E  R  S
D  I  N  C  E  P  T  I  O  N
T  H  E  C  R  E  A  T  O  R
```

Westworld, The Creator, Inception, Chappie, Terminator, Her, Star Trek, Star Wars, Ex Machina, Archive, Wall-E, Matrix, I, Robot

More

In 2023, the mass shootings continued.

more mass shootings
more common
more often

gun fetish
without
gun legislation

more bodies
more victims
more madness

a numb insanity
continues
for US

Shot through a door in 2023 . . .

Ralph Yarl, 16

wrong street
right number
looking for a sibling
when a .32 caliber
and an 84-year-old
changed his life
forever

Ajike Owens, 35

Black woman
being a Black mother
protecting her
Black children from
a White neighbor
with a gun
Karen kills

Tyre Nichols, 29

Remembering the 29-year-old Black man beaten by five Black police officers in Memphis, Tennessee on January 7, 2023. The five officers were members of the Police Department's SCORPION unit.

a somber
moment for Memphis

a Black man
defenseless

yards
away from home

attacked by a
nest of Scorpions

brothers with badges
hired Black Klansmen

it was inhumane
horrifying and insane

a senseless act
he couldn't fight back

Why?

Why Not?

Why are guns loved in this country?
Why are people around the world still hungry?

Why are the rich so rich?
Why are the poor so poor?

Why is white better than black?
Why are Black folks always under attack?

Why is Africa seen as less than?
Why no aid for the Congo and Sudan?

Why are we constantly at war?
Why have food prices continued to soar?

Why are politicians out of touch with voters?
Why can't they pass a budget by the first of October?

Why are bombs still being dropped in 2023?
Why do men want to control a woman's body?

Why is my uterus any of their business?
Why is Roe v. Wade finished?

Why are so many Black men locked up?
Why did Covid kill more of us?

Why is climate change hard to believe?
Why do we continue to cut down the trees?

Why can't we have simple gun control?
Why are teachers quitting in droves?

Why are students afraid at school?
Why are active shooter drills considered safety tools?

Why does religion seem to be more political?
Why are we angrier and more critical?

Why are folks being violent in God's name?
Why does it feel like folks are going insane?

Why is police violence an issue for us?
Why can't we drive without being nervous?

Why can't I trust the evening news?
Why is it harder to decipher the truth?

Why did so many show up on January 6th?
Why are anti-abortion supporters hypocrites?

Why are people dying at the southern border?
Why are they being bused all over?

Why has the Supreme Court lost public respect?
Why don't they have a binding code of ethics?

Why are "We the People" banning books now?
Why deny the violence about slavery and the south?

Why do white men feel so threatened?
Why do tiki torches make them feel better?

Why is Black beauty second-rate?
Why do we want to make gay men straight?

Why is social media full of lies?
Why are people who are different despised?

Why are there no real answers?
Why am I even asking these questions?

Why not?

Ohio Madness

Spotlighting Brittany Watts, a Black woman who was charged by Ohio authorities with felony abuse of a corpse after she disposed of her 21-week-old fetus.

Her water breaking too early
means a fetus died
and a mother's grief lives.

A difficult question was answered.
How do you bury your newborn child?
No laws were broken. Just a mother's heart.

The Hypocrisy

She agonized over her future as she began to regurgitate her innocence, over and over. She didn't know what to do. She was paralyzed with confusion and fear. But she had to figure it out—fast. Her future depended on it.

She sought help at a local clinic. She arrived alone. There were outraged protestors everywhere. They blocked the street and the entrance to the clinic. One White woman stood out from the rest. She was a self-proclaimed *Life Warrior*. This woman manically screamed *"Baby Killer! Baby Killer!"* over and over, while simultaneously shoving her sign in the girl's face. The sign read "Abortion is Murder." The girl was horrified by the feral energy of the woman and the crowd. Then suddenly . . . "BOOM!" Her choice was gone.

As she sat alone in an empty room several months later with a crying baby and no options, her mind played back that awful, life-altering day. There were so many wroth faces claiming that her baby was the most important thing to them. They were fighting for every unborn child—including hers.

As her baby's cry got louder and the stench of an overused diaper grew stronger, she contemplated a solution . . . *maybe, just maybe, THEY will help us.* She grabbed her wailing baby, still wrapped in the soiled diaper, and started her quest.

Her first stop was the doorstep of the man responsible for the nine minutes of horror that led to her circumstances. Her rapist. Her baby's daddy. She knocked. He answered. *"Who are you?"*

Trembling as she held up her child, the girl softly responded. *"We need help. I want life to be good for our child."*

He immediately replied, *"That's your baby, not mine."* Then he slammed the door.

Her second stop was the doorstep of the White woman shouting *"Baby Killer! Baby Killer!"* The girl knocked. The woman answered. *"Who are you?"*

Remembering the woman's rabid behavior, the girl courageously held up her child stuttering as she spoke. *"W-w-we we nee-need help. I w-w-want life to be good fffffor this child."*

The woman stood there for a minute, indifferent to their circumstances, and more annoyed that her day had been interrupted. Eventually an aloof response emerged from behind a Medusa-like stare. *"Sorry. That's your baby, not mine."* Then she walked away.

The girl continued their journey to the home of the man who tried to blow up the clinic. The girl knocked. The man answered. *"Who are you?"*

Initially the girl hesitated but eventually she held up her child repeating her plea. *"We need help. I want life to be good for this child."*

The man did not speak. He simply responded by unceremoniously closing his door.

Her next destination was the doorstep of her State Representative who voted to eliminate abortion rights. The girl knocked. The State Representative answered. *"Who are you?"*

The girl held up her child hoping that this was the one— the doorway that would change her future. *"We need help. I want life to be good for this child."*

The Representative looked around to see if anyone was watching and then replied, *"My schedule is full. Come back next week."* He briskly walked away as a staffer slowly shut the door.

Her final stop was the Supreme Court which had just

struck down the Roe v. Wade decision. The girl knocked. Three conservative justices answered. *"Who are you?"*

The girl hoisted her child so that the baby was face-to-face with the justices. This was her last chance. Her future depended on this. She took a deep breath, held it for three seconds, and then exhaled. *"We need help. I want life to be good for this child. I can't do this alone. Please help us."*

As the justices leaned over, the girl could feel the coldness of their words. *"We are not here to help mothers. We are here to change the laws."* Then they closed the door to freedom and choice.

The girl, her baby, and the soiled diaper had nowhere else to go. So, they sat solemnly on the sidewalk outside the Supreme Court building as a retinue of protestors marched dismissively past them with their godforsaken signs and vengeful chants. The baby cried. The girl cried too.

MORAL OF THE STORY:
Life does not end after birth.

Circle of Life

Exist before

Existing becomes

Eternal because

Eventually "being"

Evolves beyond

Existed becoming

Everybody's beginning

The New Kid

Recognizing the growing number of
fentanyl overdoses in this country.

There's a new kid

on the block

hiding in plain sight.

Killing with a touch.

This kid's too much.

Often not seen,

coming or going

but bodies line the path

that is left.

This kid's not natural.

This kid was created

to take you high and

to take you fast

      . . . real fast!

we need . . .   *love*

                  forgiveness

                  peace

                  patience

                  and prayer

we need . . .

                  everybody's

                  god

Our Prayer

we pray
for peace
for all,
as children live,
families die,
and whole communities are erased.

in the distance
strangers turn on strangers,
friends turn on friends,
chaos and contempt rule
as forgiveness and kindness fade
leaving a coldness and cruelty
within.

history is forgotten.
ignorance is welcomed.
violence is routine.
poverty spreads
smothering the future of so many,
as a new generation of
revolutionaries arise.

let peace be seen.
let it be heard.
let your love be felt.
guide us. protect us. forgive us.
this we pray.

amen.

Section II
The Personals

Yesterday I was clever, so I wanted to change the world. Today I am wise, so I am changing myself

--Rumi

when times are off
when I am lost and drifting at sea
i think of my mom
i think of Mississippi
i think of Brickyard Hill
i think of Yazoo City

Sisters Reunite

cause her mama was my mama
my mama was hers

mama never wanted a misunderstanding
to separate her girls

     through grief and memories

we reclaimed our sisterhood
wondering how—just how . . .

     the other misunderstood

Take Me Home

music reminds me of insouciant times
when we had nothing
and yet we had everything, coinciding
when mama was on the porch
and daddy across town
when softball games were a social oasis
and there were no neighborhood rivalries

when houses on the hill
where filled with families
when the church doors opened
pews were never empty

the first beats of a song
throwback my memories
taking me way back
taking me right back
taking me home
to my Yazoo family

music reminds me of insouciant times
when we had nothing
and yet we had everything, coinciding
the first beats of an Isley song
remind me of slow dancing with Tyrone
while the Shame of Evelyn King
reminds me of our talent show dance routine

when I hear Aretha's R-E-S-P-E-C-T
I remember the lip synch show
at Shaka's Disco
I Destroyed Your Love, Parts 1 and 2
Float On, Flashlight, & For the Love of You

the first beats of a song
throwback my memories
taking me way back
taking me right back
taking me home
to my Yazoo family

music reminds me of insouciant times
when we had nothing
and yet we had everything, coinciding
these halcyon days are anchored to my soul
I appreciate them now that so many are gone

times were special and I took them for granted
but when I hear the music
memories come flooding back
it feels so good to reminisce
for three and a half minutes
I relive my innocence

music reminds me of insouciant times
when we had nothing
and yet we had everything, coinciding
when mama was on the porch
and daddy across town
when softball games were a social oasis
and there were no neighborhood rivalries

when houses on the hill
where filled with families
when the church doors opened
pews were never empty

the first beats of a song
throwback my memories
taking me way back
taking me right back
taking me home
to my Yazoo family

When the House Went Up

Remembering my dad, Herman Leach, the first Black Yazoo County
Supervisor. He perished in a housefire on Friday, January 13, 2023.

When the house went up
A town was in shock
A family was distraught
A legacy was lost

A legacy was lost
A life was wasted
He was trapped and alone
Trapped and waiting

Trapped and waiting
For the community to come
Where is Herman?
Is he home?

Is he home?
Is he in the house?
Of course he is!
He doesn't go out

He doesn't go out
He's got to be there
Go to the back
Don't stand there and stare

Don't stand there and stare
The family did shout
Put water on the fire
Just get him out

Just get him out
He's in the back
Where's the water?
Fire Department, where you at?

Fire Department, where you at?
A hydrant is right here
Next to the house
Why look elsewhere?

Why look elsewhere?
You are wasting time
The first Black Yazoo County Supervisor
Could be dying

Could be dying
In his very own home
Cause the community he served
Left him all alone

Left him all alone
Near his back door
Lying face down
On his bathroom floor

On his bathroom floor
When the house went up
Exposing cracks in the system
For poor Black folks

For poor Black folks
He still fights
Using his death as a catalyst
For community rights

When Mama Was Down

Remembering my mother, Inell Leach, retired Headstart teacher and community activist. She passed away on Friday, July 6, 2018, after fainting at home.

When mama was down
I was not there
It was the three under the pecan tree
Trying to keep her here

She was down
She was down
far too long
Lying on a cold floor
in her very own home

They finally came
without hustle or haste
They didn't seem to care
that we had to wait

They came with
      no equipment to help
      no empathy for our distress
      no embarrassment for their tardiness
      no excuses or regrets

For their unprofessional response there was
      no apology
      no respect
      no "Sorry"
      no "Forgive us"
      nothing you would expect

Just callous behavior and
an attitude of calm
They didn't care
that she was our mom

On the side of the road
they concocted their lie
They would wait to tell the family
when she actually died

They lied to our faces
and said that the 'copter would come
Hours later
They said she was gone

Hours of prayers and fears had festered
while they lied about when she died
       . . . in the ambulance
            with no family member present

Just callous behavior and
an attitude of calm
They didn't care
that she was our mom

      They didn't care
      that she was our mom

      They didn't care

      She was our mom!

You, Yazoo #2

I blame you, Yazoo

It was
your disrespect
and your neglect
that snatched them
tossed them
and then dismissed them
without an apology or remorse

They gave so much time
that should have been mine
that's me plus three
under the pecan tree

We sacrificed
paid your price
watched them pass away
and then hear you say

without gratitude
and without truth
too bad for Herman
. . . and Inell too

I blame you, Yazoo

. . . I still blame you

On the Prowl

Dogs on the prowl
looking for fresh meat
Dogs on the prowl
without a leash
How does a young lamb survive in a land
where wild dogs roam everywhere
                    . . . trapping young lambs unaware

            Dogs at home
            Dogs at school
            Dogs on the corner
            violating rule after rule
                    . . . with some being manipulative and cruel

Dogs on the prowl
looking for fresh meat
Dogs on the prowl
without a leash
How does a young lamb survive in a land
where men act like boys
                    . . . and play with lamb toys

Dogs on the prowl
looking for fresh meat
Dogs on the prowl
while trying to teach
Dogs on the prowl
wearing fire department boots
Dogs on the prowl
wearing business suits

Dogs on the prowl
while driving a taxi
and sometimes standing in the pulpit asking
        for forgiveness and tithes
        after taking a young lamb on a late-night ride

Dogs on the prowl
wearing choir robes
Dogs on the prowl
climbing telephone poles
Wild dogs roaming everywhere
                          . . . trapping young lambs unaware

Dogs on the prowl
violating rule after rule
Generations of dogs
roaming in Yazoo

Note to Self

Your inner circle is your sanctuary. The sanctuary welcomes folks who want the best for you, who care for you, who love you, who will be there for you, who will stand up for you, who will protect you, and who will support you during the good and bad times. Folks in your inner circle care and are always there . . . even when they are not.

Keep your space clean. Eliminate the toxic folks. You know who they are. Anyone messy, angry, abusive, lazy, disrespectful, deceitful, closeminded, narrowminded, self-centered, self-righteous, critical, creepy, cruel, and/or plain crazy.

Constantly re-evaluate your inner circle. People change. You will change. Make choices. If necessary, put them out and keep them out. No one gets a spot in your inner circle based on DNA, job position, bank account, neighborhood, graduation class, social activities, or just because they want to be. A space in your inner circle is earned. It's not based on time, currency, relationship status, or position. It is based on how you feel about them.

Period.

Section III
Black Women Worthy

We often block our own blessings because we don't feel inherently good enough or smart enough or pretty enough or worthy enough…You're worthy because you are born and because you are here. Your being here, your being alive makes worthiness your birthright. You alone are enough.

—Oprah Winfrey

Being Worthy

my sisters
to be in the spotlight
to be valued
to be deserving
to be worthy

you don't have to be
more than you are

you just have to be
who you are

a Black woman
living in America

Letitia James

NY State Attorney General
on a mission for democracy.
EVICTING
the former President by
putting a spotlight on the fraud
of a fraud.
Putting him out of business
and out of NY.

AG James

Fani Willis

Fulton County top prosecutor
with a dogged reputation.
DETERMINED
to hold the former President
accountable
for his attempt
to derail democracy in Georgia.

Press on and
use your genius
to find the truth.
Make him pay.

Madam DA

Tanya Chutkan

Selected to oversee

the first

federal trial of the former President.

CLEANING UP

the January 6th mayhem.

Not afraid to hand down jail sentences.

Not afraid to

    . . . lock them up!

Judge Chutkan

Angel Reese

LSU basketball beauty
confident and talented
with her ring finger
she stirred up

CONTROVERSY

exposing another double standard
for Black women.
She is a young Black woman
on a path to athletic greatness.

Bayou Barbie

Coco Gauff

Next generation
tennis star.
Breakthrough
championship
that was hard played
and then
because she prayed
CONTROVERSY
was conveyed.
She was underrated
leaving some frustrated
with her win.
Raised on a foundation of faith
thank you was her prayer.

She's an athlete,
a young Black woman
poised and prepared
for greatness.
She's a 19-year-old
U. S. Open Champion

ShaCarrie Richardson

Next generation
track star.
One of the fastest women
in history at age 19.

Her journey was a
CONTROVERSY
that she had to overcome.
Stress and grief
only made her stronger
and faster.

Now, she's an athlete,
a young Black woman
sprinting right into
greatness.

World Champion

Tasha Smith

is a director, producer, mentor
who's always acting up.

Always acting . . .
like Brenda's running out of time
like Angela didn't get married too
like Carol wasn't drugged and lost in Empire
like Ronnie wasn't on The Corner
like she couldn't survive the thickest moments
like she had Game and that she did it for All of Us
like Chicago had hope
like Boston was common
like Daddy's Little Girls were Addicted
and like she's a Star in Bad Boys 4.
For Better or Worse,

Tasha Smith
is a director, producer, mentor
who's always acting up.

She is a Black woman
on a journey
to cinematic greatness.

Karine Jean-Pierre

White House Press Secretary

and political advisor

facing the cameras.

HISTORIC

Black woman openly

stepping up to the podium.

A Black woman openly

answering the hard questions.

Strong Voice

Jasmine Crockett

Watchout! She's coming!

The new sheriff in town

is a Texas congresswoman

wearing many hats for those in need.

REPRESENTING

a new generation of leadership.

She is a Black woman speaking up,

a Black woman speaking out

to protect our democracy.

Congresswoman Crockett

Beyonce Carter

The Queen B

of entertainment.

Her greatest achievement

was a marathon of music and athletics. Her

RENAISSANCE WORLD TOUR

was a cultural event

openly welcoming all

and now . . .

she is country.

Cowboy Carter

Tracy Chapman

First black woman
to win a CMA award
for her signature hit.
        35 years later
        climbing the charts.
        Thanks to Luke Combs
                FAST CAR
                moved quickly
                to no. 1 on Billboard's
                country music chart.
                A song and singer
                that are just . . .

                Timeless

Shannon Nash

She is one of the most influential,

Helping future financial leaders

Advance. She is the mother of an autistic son who

Needed quality childcare. She also

Noticed that Black women were missing from boards.

ONBOARD is her documentary which highlights the low

Number of Black female board members.

No corporate boards were

Actually looking for us, and vice versa

She is one of Silicon Valley's most influential

Helping corporate boards become more diverse.

Dawn Staley

From college player
to the WNBA player;
to Olympic gold;
to college coach.
This South Carolina
GAMECOCKS

history maker is . . .
Naismith Player of the Year
Naismith Coach of the Year
a WNBA All-Star
a Hall of Fame inductee.

This history maker has . . .
multiple SEC regular season championships
multiple national titles
an amazing undefeated season
and one of the most recognizable
and respected
faces in the game.

She's our
"Boo"

Autumn Lockwood

Making sports history.
The first of her kind.
Black woman coaching in
SUPER BOWL LVII

Black woman
making coaching history
as a City of Brotherly Love,
as a Philadelphia Eagles
Assistant Coach

Kimberly Jones

Driven by her students.
Throwing English parties.
Giving lifelong skills
at Chapel Hill.

North Carolina

2023

TEACHER OF THE YEAR

A Black woman
unlocking potential
in every student.

CONGRATULATIONS!

Brittany Bonnaffons

Using Algebra to defy the odds.
Helping students LEAP over challenges.

Louisiana

2023

TEACHER OF THE YEAR

Also directing students
to become a better version of themselves.
In Luling, she connects and
coaches champions.

CONGRATULATIONS!

Candice Jackson

Guiding third graders
in Detroit Public Schools.
Helping students achieve potential.

Michigan

2023

TEACHER OF THE YEAR

Empowering fellow educators.
A Black woman
uplifting her community.

CONGRATULATIONS!

Chevell Simeon

15-year career
at public and private schools.
Helping students achieve potential.

St. Thomas-St. John
2023
TEACHER OF THE YEAR

Believing in the uniqueness of
every student.
A Black woman
encouraging students to explore
through hands-on experience.

CONGRATULATIONS!

Others

many more to lift

like sunrise over a lake

their rays expose truth

Recognizing the multitude of Black women who are worthy.

Reserved for reader reflections . . .
Write-in the name of a Black woman who is worthy.

The Reader Spotlight

*We can talk about making a difference
or we can make a difference.*

--Anonymous

In the Light

Everyday deeds
Ordinary women shine
Doing what they do

Fame is a stranger
Hard work is the foundation
Black women are rocks

Denise Robertson
First Lady of New King Solomon Church
Yazoo City, MS

Denise is the first African American Tax Assessor for Yazoo County, Mississippi. She has also served at the national level as a volunteer for the International Association of Assessing Officers. She married Rev. Dr. Gregory Robertson, long-time pastor of New King Solomon Church, and worked by his side in the church for over 15 years until he passed away in January 2023. Today Denise continues her work in the church without her loving and dedicated husband, and spiritual leader. In 2023 she was re-elected as the county's Tax Assessor for a second term.

Denise
(perseverance)

A waterfall falls
with beauty, strength, and purpose
. . . even in darkness

Julia Brown Karimu
Retired Co-Executive of Global Ministries

In 1990 Julia was ordained by the Christian Church (Disciples of Christ) where she served with general ministries for 44 years. In 1996, the Christian Church and United Church of Christ established *Global Ministries*. Julia was there throughout the whole process and was instrumental in building the *Global Ministries* partnership.

In 2011, Julia was President of the Division of Overseas Ministries and Co-Executive of Global Ministries. During her tenure, she established area initiatives that helped people in key areas around the world, including the Congo and the Middle East. In December 2021, Julia retired from her position. At that point, the church established the *Julia Brown Karimu Fund* as a permanent reminder of her global contributions.

Julia
(vision)

A mountaintop view
does not change with the seasons
Wow! I am so small

Sister Maalikah Muhammad
Entrepreneur, owner of
"Kameelah's Closet"

Sister Maalikah has always been a strong leader and advocate for women. She has always lived with an entrepreneurial spirit. Some of her many business ventures include "Black Like Me" (hand-painted tee-shirt dresses), "Bean Pie Express," "Your University" (MUI affiliate school), "Suite Baby Cakes" (gourmet pastry business), "A Second Glance" (editing services), and most recently the world-renowned "Kameelah's Closet" (modest fashion wear). She is inspired by the idea of providing services that our people need and doing it with integrity. Some of the lessons that she has learned through her leadership in the Nation of Isam and as a businesswoman include: 1) *"find a need and fill it,"* 2) *"operate with integrity,"* and 3) *"a satisfied customer is far greater than profit."*

Maalikah
(optimism)

Dark clouds paint the sky
Lightning strikes and thunder rolls
You prefer rainbows

Pastor Annette Alvizures
Co-Pastor of "A Place of Refuge International Ministries"
LaGrange, Georgia

Annette has diligently worked for over 36 years, 10 years military and 26 years government, doing what she loves most—helping others. God has opened many doors for her to travel, meet, and touch the lives of people from all over the world while sharing her love for God. While assigned to Shaw Airforce Base in South Carolina, she accepted her calling and was licensed as an evangelist in 2009. She was ordained in October of 2011.

Her outreach consisted of ministering in nursing homes, prisons, various retreats, and conferences. She mentored and coached locally and globally with outreach work in Kenya and the Philippines. She is the Founder of Healing, Empowerment, Enrichment, and Teaching (HEET) International Ministries. In 2022, she was elevated to the title of pastor, and she now serves as a co-pastor with her husband, Pastor Ruben Alvizures.

Annette
(faith)

Raindrops fall quickly
You look to heaven slowly
Hmmm! You are not wet

Dr. Gloria Lindsey-Tate
Mississippi Area Coordinator for the Southeastern Region
of Sigma Gamma Rho Incorporated
(1960 – 2023)

Gloria was a beloved wife, mother, and educator, who devoted her life to God and serving others. She proudly served as the Mississippi Area Coordinator for the Southeastern Region of Sigma Gamma Rho Sorority Incorporated, from the year 2020 to 2023. Her journey with Sigma Gamma Rho began with the Alpha Tau Chapter at Jackson State University in the spring of 1982. She later became a charter member of the Mu Iota Sigma Alumnae Chapter of Desoto County, MS, and served as the Inaugural Basileus in 2016. Two scholarships in support of Jackson State University and Sigma Gamma Rho Sorority have been established in honor of her life and legacy. She will be remembered.

Gloria
(legacy)

A yellow tea rose
blooming on a warm spring day
Always remembered

*And whatever you ask in prayer,
you will receive, if you have faith.*

—Matthew 21:22

Acknowledgements

The poems in this book reflect the personal opinions of the author. I acknowledge that I am a "Pro Choice" supporter. I

believe that a woman should have full control of her body. The decision to carry a child to term, or not, is difficult enough. She does not need men or the legal system intervening in her personal care and criminalizing her every move.

Losing my father in a housefire in 2023 was a traumatic event for my family, and so was the unexpected passing of my mother in 2018. I honestly believe that if they had been afforded quality city services, then a greater chance of survival would have been likely for both. As I have done on multiple occasions, I have chosen to use my poetry to express my feelings. It has been over five years since my mother was called home. Yet she continues to be the inspiration for my poetry. It is her memory and her love that keep me praying and writing. Thank you, Mama!

Dr. Gloria Lindsey-Tate was one of my "Big Sisters" when I pledged Sigma Gamma Rho Sorority at Jackson State University. It was two of us pledging, Dorothy and Revonne. It can be challenging to be part of a small line on a university campus, but Gloria made the whole experience less stressful. She was always sharing kind words, always attentive to our needs, and always reassuring us that we would be great sorors someday. Sadly, Gloria passed away in 2023, but her legacy will live on through her friends, her family, and our sorority. Thank you, "Big Sister Gloria," for being a role model, a sister, and a friend.

Not all *Dear Black Woman Reader Spotlight* recipients are included in this book. For the complete list of past and present *Reader Spotlight* honorees, please go to my author website, www.revonnejohnsonbooks.com.

The statistic related to global warming was taken from the following website:

Jacobs, Peter, Karen Fox and Katherine Rohloff. *NASA Analysis Confirms 2023 as Warmest Year on Record*. Greenbelt, 24 January 2024. <https://www.nasa.gov/news-release/nasa-analysis-confirms-2023-as-warmest-year-on-record/>.

The Teacher of the Year awards were taken from the following websites:

Daily News Staff. (2023, December 15). *The Virgin Islands Daily News*. Retrieved from Chevell Simeon is Teacher of the Year for St. Thomas-St. John District: https://www.virginislandsdailynews.com/news/chevell-simeon-is-teacher-of-the-year-for-st-thomas-st-john-district/article_6f61ac57-b619-59fb-9184-4273868e4c86.html

Marzell, T. L. (2023, April 13). *Brittany Bonnaffons named Louisiana's 2023 Teacher of the Year*. Retrieved from Chalkboard Champions: https://chalkboardchampions.org/brittany-bonnaffons-named-louisianas-2023-teacher-of-the-year/

McClellan, H. V. (2023, April 14). *Kimberly Jones of Chapel Hill named N.C.'s 2023 Teacher of the Year*. Retrieved from EdNC: https://www.ednc.org/04-14-2023-kimberly-jones-of-chapel-hill-named-n-c-s-2023-teacher-of-the-year/

Media Contact Public and Governmental Affairs. (2023, May 04). *Detroit Third Grade Teacher Named Michigan Teacher of the Year*. Retrieved from Michigan Department of Education: https://www.michigan.gov/mde/news-and-information/press-releases/2023/05/04/detroit-third-grade-teacher-named-michigan-teacher-of-the-year

About the Author

Revonne Johnson has written poetry off and on since high school. She is a wife, a parent, a community volunteer, and an Information Technology professional. She published her first poem when she partnered with her sister to create the *Legends Poetry* series. Her solo projects include a memoir about her high school basketball team, and the *Dear Black Woman* poetry collection. Please see her author's website for more information about all her writing projects.

www.revonnejohnsonbooks.com

Made in the USA
Columbia, SC
08 July 2024